NEW SPORTS HEROES FOR GIRLS

Sword of a Champion

The Story of Sharon Monplaisir

by Doreen and Michael Greenberg,
based on interviews with the athlete

Illustrations by Phil Velikan

Wish Publishing
Terre Haute, Indiana
www.wishpublishing.com

LCCN: 00-102419

Book edited by Rick Frey
Cover designed by Phil Velikan
Front cover photo from the collection of Sharon Monplaisir
Proofread by Heather Lowhorn

Printed in the United States of America
10 9 8 7 6 5 4 3 2 1

Published in the United States by
Wish Publishing
P.O. Box 10337
Terre Haute, IN 47801, USA
www.wishpublishing.com

Distributed in the United States by
Cardinal Publishers Group
Indianapolis, Indiana 46240

Acknowledgments

The lifelong dedication of Carole Oglesby, Mariah Burton Nelson and Donna Lopiano to the promotion of women in sports has inspired us to write the Anything You Can Do... series. We'd like to thank the Women's Sports Foundation for its support and in particular the efforts of Yolanda Jackson.

Deepest thanks go to our editor Rick Frey who shared our vision to promote new heroes for young girls.

We are indebted to Michael Cohen, Jordan Shapiro, Arthur Seidel and Diann Cohen for their most helpful comments and criticisms.

Daniel Kron of SportsforWomen.com has been a wonderful resource and supportive friend.

Special thanks to Michael Gostigian and Eric Rosenberg for reminiscing with us about Sharon's life.

We are forever grateful to our beautiful daughters, Alice and Jane, for their patience, example, advice and love.

We have always marveled, along with everyone else, at the awe-inspiring achievements of Jackie Joyner-Kersee and Julie Foudy. We are very proud that their insightful comments are part of our series.

Above all, we must thank Sharon, the hero of this book. Her talent, dedication and courage make her an example to readers young and old.

Finally, we wish to acknowledge the young girls who run and swim and shoot baskets and fence and play tennis and kick soccer balls and water ski and hit softballs. You look to the athletes who came before you for your inspiration. We look to you for the future.

Any errors of fact or omission are solely the responsibility of the authors. Michael believes that the mistakes are due to Doreen, and Doreen believes that they must be Michael's fault.

Doreen & Michael Greenberg

"I think little girls need to have big girls to look up to!"

*– Teresa Edwards, Five-time Olympian
& professional basketball player*

Contents

Dear Reader,

The story of Sharon Monplaisir is one of a series of exciting, true stories about female athletes. Sharon grew up very poor in a tough neighborhood of New York City. She had few friends and was often teased by the kids at school. In high school Coach Fine showed her how the sport of fencing could open up an exciting new world and allow Sharon to overcome her fears. Sharon would go on to become an All-American champion and three-time Olympic athlete. Her life is an inspiration to young girls interested in the world of sports.

Doreen & Michael Greenberg

• • •

Dear Parent and Teacher,

Sharon Monplaisir's story is one of courage and inspiration. We invite you to read along and discuss with the young reader the circumstances of Sharon's life. We know that participation in exercise and sports can bring many rewards to young girls including a higher sense of self-esteem and positive relationships with others. This is also an opportunity to engage in a discussion of those frustrations and anxieties that young athletes face at any level of competition.

We have attempted to raise some of the social and personal issues that girls and young women often confront every day. You are an important part of the process. Explore together. Read together. Talk together. Possible discussion questions, issues and resources can be found at the end of the book in the "Sports Talk" section. BEST OF ALL, Sharon's story is optimistic and enthralling and a lot of fun to read.

Doreen & Michael Greenberg

Preface

by Julie Foudy

When I was in elementary school, all of my brothers' friends called me Jimmy, because I was such a tomboy. I loved watching football and playing touch football. I loved watching the Los Angeles Lakers basketball team — those guys were my heroes... Magic, Worthy and Kareem. I would watch them dunk the ball and block shots. I wanted to emulate them, but a five-foot tall girl had a hard time dunking the ball. I didn't have a Mia Hamm to watch on television. I didn't have a Jennifer Azzi to watch in the WNBA. And for sure, I did not have a Women's World Cup Soccer to watch on TV.

One of the lasting images of the Women's World Cup will be all the little girls watching women performing great feats in front of great crowds — painted faces and all. My special memory is an image of the huge smiles on all those painted faces. A dream became a reality. These same little girls are now thinking, "Hey, if Mia, Michele and Julie can do it, I can do it." Now, they are not only dreaming about a World Cup Trophy or an Olympic medal, they are believing in it.

For this reason precisely, all of us on the U.S. National Soccer Team realize the importance of being role models. We cherish the fact that we truly can make a difference in the lives of these children. We see it every day in their eyes and on their faces. We tell them to watch, to learn, and most importantly, to believe. If we can do it — they can do it. The reaction we get from them says it all... a huge smile and a high five.

JULIE FOUDY was a member and co-captain of the U.S. National Team that won the 1999 Federation Internationale de Football (FIFA) Women's World Cup. An 11-year veteran of the team, Foudy earned a gold medal in 1998 at the Goodwill Games. Foudy also was a captain of the U.S. National Team that won a gold medal at the 1996 Olympic Games and competed for the United States in the 1995 FIFA Women's World Cup, in which her team finished third. Foudy was a four-time NCAA All-American at Stanford University and was voted Most Valuable Player in 1989, 1990 and 1991. She was also a finalist for the Hermann Trophy in 1991 and 1992. Foudy is currently the President-Elect of the Women's Sports Foundation.

Introduction

by Jackie Joyner-Kersee

More than 25 years ago, the Women's Sports Foundation was founded to promote the lifelong participation of girls and women in sports and fitness. We have been very successful, and we have seen many changes over the years. At that time only one in 27 girls played sports; now it's one in three. And that's because more and more opportunities exist to be a female athlete and also to follow female sports heroes.

Even with thousands of girls attending World Cup Soccer or cheering on their favorite WNBA team, we still have a long way to go. We need to get the message out to more girls. We need to let every girl know how great it feels to play sports and how very important it is to her whole being. We still have too many 11- and 12-year-old girls dropping out of sports or never even having had the chance to play at all. In fact, if a girl does not participate in sports by age 10, there is a less than 10-percent chance that she will be participating when she is 25.

Research suggests that girls who participate in sports have a real advantage over girls who do not.

Girls active in sports are more likely to be successful in school, less likely to get involved with drugs, and less likely to have an unwanted pregnancy. Sport and exercise can help to keep girls healthy, both physically and emotionally. The girl who is athletic feels stronger, eats and sleeps better, is more self-confident, and generally feels more positive about her life.

For a very long time, boys have had unlimited resources, such as books, movies, and games about sports and their favorite sports legends. Sport is where boys have traditionally learned about achieving, goal-setting, teamwork and the pursuit of excellence. Girls and women should have these skills, too. We need to establish a large-scale network of resources about girls' sports and female athletes.

And we need to give girls their own heroes. "Anything You Can Do..." is unprecedented in its concept of offering real stories of new heroes to young girls. These are the adventures of young girls coming from different backgrounds who go on to achieve excellence in sports.

This series can open a whole new world for young girls. These books will give young girls a chance to explore the biographies of elite female athletes and their early sport experiences. The common thread that runs through all of these stories is a strong one — of perseverance and desire. Yet, each story is unique. Some are famous; some are not. Although the young reader may not always recognize the name of every athlete in the series, she may very well recognize herself, her friends and her teammates in these stories.

Doreen and Michael Greenberg bring to this series a long dedication to providing positive sport experiences for girls. I like their philosophy that it is not as important for the young reader to come away with the name of the person who won the big championship or the winning score, as an understanding of what it means to be a female athlete.

And by including the unique "Sports Talk" section in each book, Doreen has the opportunity to use her expertise as a sport psychology consultant and researcher to discuss important issues with parents and teachers. These are issues distinctive to girls in sports, including competing with the boys, making sacrifices, dealing with coaches, anxieties about winning and losing, and concerns about body image.

I am delighted that these books deal with a young girl's introduction to sports, the highs and lows of training and competition, and the reactions of family and friends, both positive and negative. It is so important for all of us to understand the young athlete as a complete person.

Most of all, the books in this series are fun and exciting to read. They will inspire girls to follow their dreams — whatever they are.

JACKIE JOYNER-KERSEE was widely considered to be the best all-around female athlete in sports when she became the first woman to win back-to-back Olympic gold medals in the heptathlon at the 1988 and 1992 Olympic Games. The heptathlon is a grueling event in which athletes contest seven different events (100-meters, 100-meter hurdles, high jump, javelin, 200-meters, long jump and 800-meters) over the course of two days. A pulled hamstring forced her out of the heptathlon competition at the 1996 Olympic Games, but she came back to capture a bronze medal in the long jump. She also won a gold medal in the long jump at the 1988 Olympic Games, a silver medal in the heptathlon at the 1984 Olympic Games and a bronze in the long jump at the 1992 Olympic Games. She still holds the world record for the heptathlon of 7,291 points, which she set in 1988 at the Seoul Olympics.

1

First Touch

Sharon stands in front of the door. She reads the hand-lettered sign for about the millionth time. Taking a deep breath, she hesitates. Sharon looks right and left to see if any of her classmates are watching. "You're too skinny," they would tease. "Fencing's just for boys! "

She stares at her reflection in the frosted glass. Maybe they were right, she thinks. Maybe she didn't really belong. Maybe fencing was just too hard for someone like her. Pushing her big glasses back up on her nose, she reads the sign again:

> Anyone interested in joining the Fencing Team, Stop by the boys' gym office and see Mr. Fine

Sharon had been at this door last year. She had walked down the dark hallway, past the broken lockers and the walls where kids had spray-painted their names, to this office door. But last year she was afraid to go in.

Lakewood Memorial Library
Lakewood, New York 14750

Now, one month before her 16th birthday, Sharon is ready to go in and see Mr. Fine. There is something about fencing — something about becoming part of a team.

Sharon does not know that opening this door will change her whole life. How could she? She only knows what has led her to this door, again. She reaches for the doorknob.

• • •

Sometimes Sharon felt old. Even at age 8, she knew things that most kids didn't know. She knew all about scary things and scary people. She understood who to trust and who to stay away from.

Life in the South Bronx section of New York City was not easy. The six-floor apartment building that Sharon lived in was part of public housing. The elevator almost never worked. There were a lot of things they didn't have. Sometimes there was no heat or electricity or hot water. But there were always plenty of mice. And there was lots of noise in the hallways all the time.

Each day was a challenge. The trick was to get to school and back home again safely. You couldn't just stay out and play. The streets were too dangerous. There were kids buying and selling drugs on the corner.

There were always kids at the playground ready for a fight. The "bad guys" in her world were real.

It made Sharon tough.

Sharon would imagine a life like the ones she saw on T.V. She would dream of sitting at a table with a family and eating a big dinner. There was no father at her table. She never knew her dad. There was only her mom and her big sister, Sheila.

Sharon's favorite cartoon on T.V. was "Johnny Quest." He would go on great adventures to far away places. He had a best friend, Hadji, and a little dog. In this make-believe world, children had a mom and a dad, lots of fun things to do, and a nice place to live.

"Do you think I'll ever get to go on great adventures like Johnny and Hadji?" Sharon asked her mom one night, her voice filled with excitement. Sharon's mom did not answer. She was tired from working hard all day long, and now she was standing bent over the ironing board. She was pressing the skirt that Sharon had worn to school that day, so that she would look nice at class tomorrow.

"I'd like to travel all over the world and meet lots of nice new people and speak in different languages." Sharon's mom grumbled something in reply. She didn't know very many people born in this neighborhood who had ever left the South Bronx. And, to tell the truth, most of those who did leave had never come to much good.

"Can I Mom? Can I go on an adventure and travel all around the world?" asked Sharon.

"Stranger things have happened, I guess," mumbled Sharon's mom, almost to herself. Then she went back to her ironing.

Sharon had to share a room with Sheila. It was very plain. There were no pictures on the walls. She didn't have a toy chest filled with pretty dolls. She didn't have shelves of books and fun games. Still, she tried to keep her little corner clean and neat. Sharon really didn't have enough things to make it messy. Sometimes she would sleep in the living room. It was usually warmer in there.

In the apartment next door was another mom with two children. She was always very nice to Sharon. She would let Sharon come in when her mom didn't get home in time and Sharon didn't have any place to go. Sometimes she would have Sharon join them for dinner — for the best spaghetti and meatballs. Sharon would always remember the nice neighbor lady and the great spaghetti with the crumbly meatballs in the sauce.

It seemed to Sharon that her own mom wasn't very happy about being a mom, or maybe she just wasn't able to do the things that most moms did. Sharon had no other relatives nearby — no aunt or grandmother to make her feel part of a family. Her big sister Sheila tried to be like a mom to Sharon. It was Sheila who would protect her. Sharon would run to her when the other kids picked on her. And they would pick on her a lot.

They would tease her about her awkward looks and her hand-me-down clothes. She was always wearing the same red plaid dress. She only had one dress. She was tall and skinny with these big glasses that the other kids said made her look like a bug. Sharon did have a pretty smile, but often there wasn't much to smile about.

Sheila would read to Sharon all the time. Sharon loved to hear stories over and over again. Her big sister had a great imagination and would make all the stories come alive for her.

The best stories were about the Greek warriors and goddesses who lived long, long ago. They were strong and brave and battled horrible monsters. But in the end, they would always win. Again and again Sharon begged Sheila to tell her the story of the wonderful goddess Athena. Athena stood side by side with all-powerful Zeus and mighty Hercules, with a great golden sword in her hand. On the sunlit beaches of that ancient world, they fought the evil giants.

In Sharon's imagination she would become Athena. Of course, she wouldn't be skinny any more, but very strong. And she would have lovely golden robes that everyone admired. "Someday, I'm going to fight with a magic sword," Sharon told her sister Sheila. "I'll be strong and brave, and thousands of people will cheer when I win."

Sheila looked down at her little sister and shook

her head. "You're just a dreamer," Sheila said.

"But what's wrong with dreaming anyway?" Sharon asked. "I love to dream."

Sheila looked lovingly at Sharon. She looked around the apartment room and then up at the ceiling, so Sharon wouldn't see the big wet tears in her sad brown eyes. "Nothing," said Sheila. "There's nothing at all wrong with dreaming."

Sharon would think about these great adventures every night as she cuddled under her blanket to keep warm. After a while, the noises in the hall and on the street would fade away, and she could fall asleep.

● ● ●

The sirens screamed. The lights flashed. Sharon jumped out of bed and ran to the window in the living room. She saw the enormous red fire truck speeding down the street. The men on the back of the engine held on tightly as the truck screeched around the corner. The firemen had become her true-life heroes. They stood tall in their black helmets and shiny yellow coats. They were brave. They would save anybody. It did not matter who you were. Sharon waved and called out to the firemen as they went by.

The sirens in the night and the flashing lights and the brave men were so exciting. In the morning, on her way to school, Sharon would see another burned-out building down the street. Broken glass and charred bricks were all around. Dirty ice clogged the gutters.

"Why were there so many fires?" Sharon asked herself. She lived in an upside-down world. The nighttime was full of explosions of color and excitement; the daytime was just dreary, bleak and sad.

Often, Sheila would take her little sister on long walks — past the playground and underneath the tracks of the elevated train. As they walked along, hand in hand, Sheila would play story-games with Sharon to pass the time.

Sharon's favorite story-game was the "magic rock." Sheila would find a round rock with a pointy end in the park. She would throw this magic rock and they would run to see where it landed. They would look to see what direction it was pointing.

Which ever way it pointed — that is where their "adventure" would take them. It always pointed away from home. They would run and run together. They were just like Johnny Quest and Hadji. Sharon loved running through the park and down the city streets. She felt strong. She felt happy.

Sometimes, Sheila would pretend that they were lost, but she really knew the way home — back to the cold dingy apartment building. She also knew that any happiness Sharon would have in life would be away from the streets of the South Bronx — in another world altogether. But Sharon loved these adventures in which she thought they were going so far away.

Sharon didn't really have any best friends. Many of the kids would pick on her because her clothes were old and out of style, or because she was too skinny with long arms and legs — like a praying mantis. She was told by her mom to come straight home after school. The neighborhood was too dangerous. There was no chance to visit and play with classmates. She was much too ashamed to ask kids to come back to her small shabby apartment.

• • •

School was the best part of the day. In a way, the teachers became her best friends. They liked Sharon because she was nice and quiet and always interested in learning. She worked hard in school to do her very best. Sharon did well in school. She especially liked reading. She would ask permission to take classroom books home. Sharon would spend hours and hours reading the stories again and again. After Sheila left home, the books kept Sharon company during the lonely evening hours.

In junior high, Sharon liked biology the most. She learned all about plants and animals. She studied the drawings in her textbook that showed all of the parts of the body. She knew all the names of the important organs — the heart, the lungs and all the muscles.

One day, Sharon was asked to become the biology

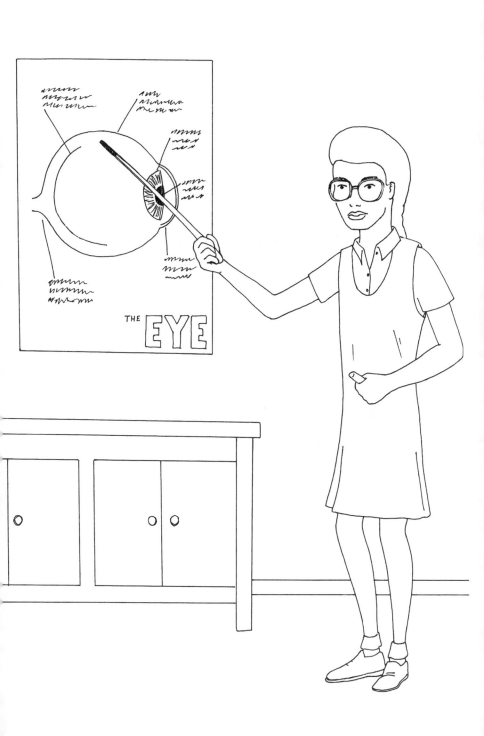

THE EYE

assistant and to help the teacher do experiments and special projects. She would stand in front of the class and point to the parts of the body on the anatomy chart. She liked the extra responsibility. She would carefully write the names on the blackboard. It was nice to know that her abilities were seen by others.

Sometimes a teacher would make a special effort to be a friend to Sharon. There was Mrs. Anton, the English teacher, who knew that Sharon loved the stories they read in class. Also, there was a very nice young French teacher who always stayed a few minutes after school to spend some time with Sharon. She would listen to Sharon and talk about whatever was on Sharon's mind that day. It was nice to have a grown-up so interested in what she was doing and what she was thinking.

Maybe one day Sharon could be a teacher, too. She could live in a warm apartment, in a nice building with lots of books to read. The people there would be friendly, too. When she would meet them in the hallway or in the elevator, they would always smile and say, "Hello, how are you today?"

How very sad Sharon was when she came to class one day and heard that her French teacher would not be returning to her school. She had been knocked down and badly hurt by a gang of high school kids on her way home from school. The meanness of the streets had found its way even into the safe shelter of the school.

Sharon thought that she was tough enough to take whatever troubles life brought her. But as she sat at her desk, big warm tears washed down her cheeks. Sharon felt horrible. Maybe things would be better when she started high school in the fall. Maybe she would make a new friend. Maybe the kids wouldn't tease her so much. Sharon hoped she would be happier there, but she had learned that it was better not to expect too much.

● ● ●

Math class was never Sharon's favorite at Theodore Roosevelt High School. One day, while sitting in math, her mind was wandering like it sometimes did. She thought about the sign she had seen earlier in the day. It was about joining the fencing team. Mr. Fine had posted it all around the school. She began to think about it. She didn't like going home. Sharon always wanted to find something to do after school, so that she wouldn't have to go home right away.

She had tried basketball, and although she was a good shooter, she wasn't very good at dribbling the ball. The girls on Roosevelt's basketball team seemed rough and nasty to her. The swim team was out — she was only good at sinking in the water. She had never really had a chance to learn.

Sharon loved to run, and she thought about going out for the track and field team. But the kids there looked so much bigger and stronger. She watched the powerful way that they jumped the hurdles and raced around the track. Nobody seemed to pay any attention to the girl standing on the side with the nervous look on her face.

She had thought about fencing last year, when Mr. Fine and the fencing students had put up the announcement around the school.

This time Sharon would do it! She walked quickly down the hall to Mr. Fine's door. She was excited to join the fencing team. She turned the knob and walked in. Sharon Monplaisir could not know that she was about to begin her most exciting adventure of all.

2

En Garde

The first thing that Sharon noticed about Mr. Fine was his soft voice. He was very tall, with jet-black hair and a mustache, but it was his nice quiet voice that caught her attention.

" Have you ever fenced before? " Mr. Fine asked Sharon.

"No," Sharon answered.

"Have you ever seen fencing?" asked Mr. Fine.

Sharon replied, "Yes, sort of, I'm not sure..."

Mr. Fine smiled, "Okay, stop by tomorrow for practice and see if you like it."

The next day, in the late afternoon, Sharon went to the little room off of the main gym room, that was known as "The Fencing Room." It was a long narrow room with tan walls and a dark wooden floor. Although the fencers called this the fencing room, she could see by the big mats pushed off to the side that this was also "The Wrestling Room." The old pommel horse and uneven bars in the corner meant that for the gymnasts this was also "The Gymnastics Room." This space was to become Sharon's room as well.

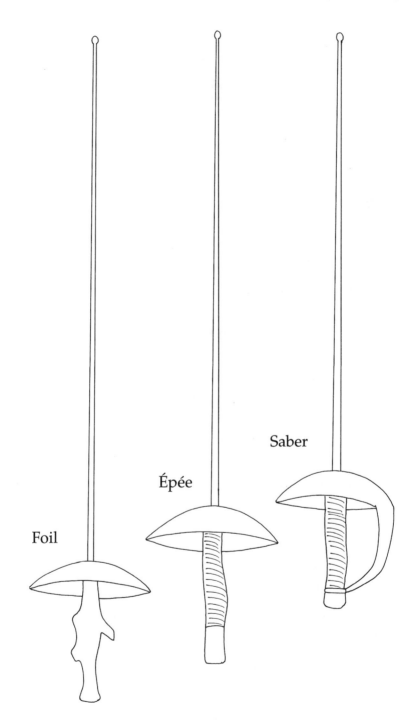

Foil

Épée

Saber

Sharon walked in. She saw Mr. Fine giving a lesson to one of the students. They looked like they were fighting each other with swords. He looked up and saw Sharon. There was his smile again. All the other gym teachers would yell all the time. They had to — most of the kids were pretty bad in class. But not Mr. Fine. He never yelled, and mistakes were no big deal to him. Even the bad kids respected Mr. Fine.

There were 10 kids involved in various activities — all new and strange to her. These activities would become part of her daily life. Some were holding swords in their hands and practicing touching the proper target area with the point of the weapon. There were kids doing a strange exercise with their feet — going back and forth in a straight line. It looked funny to Sharon, like some weird dance.

"It's called footwork," said Mr. Fine. "It's an important part of fencing, and we do that a lot in training" he said, coming over to greet Sharon.

He asked one of the students to hand him his weapon. He held it out for Sharon to inspect. He explained that this sword with its long, skinny blade is called a foil. He told her that there are three kinds of swords used in fencing. There was the foil, the épée, and the saber. They all came from different weapons of combat. Sharon learned that this was how soldiers fought duels hundreds of years ago.

The sword that they used in high school competitions was the foil. Sharon would have to learn a lot about this weapon. She would have to learn how to hold it and move really fast with it. She would have to learn how to aim it and touch the target area on the other person. She would have to learn how to escape being touched by the other person's foil.

Mr. Fine called George over. George was a senior on the team. Mr. Fine introduced Sharon and asked George to show her some fencing moves. George began to describe the world of fencing competition to Sharon.

George explained that fencing is always two people dueling each other. The object of the game is to touch and not be touched. The winner is the fencer who gets the right number of touches first in a bout. The bout is the timed, scored match in a competition. The first person to score five points is the winner. If no one scores five points in four minutes, whoever has the most points is the winner.

You get points by making a hit, touching the end of your blade on a target area on your opponent's body. For foil fencing, the target area is the torso or trunk of the body. The target area does not include the head or the arms or legs.

Sharon watched two of the students doing this. It looked like a fast dance with people trying to stab each other with swords. In practice and training sessions, two students would pretend to be rivals, or opponents, each trying to win points. The first person would make an attack by stretching out the arm and continuing to try to hit the other person. To stop the touch from hitting, the other fencer would parry to prevent the attack and then make an attack. Then the first person would make a counterattack.

This was how Sharon first learned all the techniques — from the older kids on the team. There were a lot of rules and skills to learn, too. It looked like hard work.

George handed Sharon one of the foil weapons. She had to grab it by the handle, or grip, and hold it straight out. The weapon must be held and used with only one hand. Although it is the lightest of the fencing weapons — with its long, flexible steel blade — it felt heavy and awkward in her hand. George showed her how to grab hold with just the thumb and the pointer finger. He demonstrated how to stand in the proper position, with her heels touching and her feet making an "L". George was very patient with her.

Sharon noticed that George didn't give her funny looks or make any nasty comments about how she was dressed. As a matter of fact, all the kids at fencing practice were real nice. They didn't seem to care that all she had to wear were her old blue sneakers and her light blue bell-bottom pants that were too short for her. The kids in her other classes would pick on her about her "high-water" pants.

"Thanks for not making a big deal about these

funny old clothes," Sharon said to George.

George laughed, "To tell you the truth, I never really noticed. I guess we all look a little goofy in these old uniforms and big fencing masks," he said. "But I did notice that you're catching on really fast. It's nice to have you on the team."

Sharon smiled. Not only were the fencers friendly, but Sharon soon figured out that they were also the smarter students with the better grades at school.

• • •

In one month, Sharon was coming to fencing team practice every day. Mr. Fine saw how quickly she was learning all the skills. He started giving Sharon early morning lessons every day. Sharon came to the fencing gym at 7 o'clock in the morning before school and stayed after school for practice.

Sharon soon learned what hard work it was. In fencing she would have to use all the muscles of her body, and all her muscles ached! Her body had to get used to the tough training. She had to learn how to stand in the fencing position for long periods at a time. It was like sitting in a chair — with her feet apart, knees bent, and back held very straight — but without the chair!

Sharon loved the way she got to move quickly trying to hit her opponent. She had to learn how to get her eye and hand and foot movements all going at the same time. She had to pay careful attention to what her opponent was doing and to respond with her own moves. Deciding what move to make was an important skill to learn.

Sharon was surprised when Mr. Fine asked her to practice against the older boys on the team.

"Speed is more important than size in our sport," said Coach Fine. "Balance is more important than strength."

Sharon thought about what Coach Fine was telling her. She was starting to believe that if she continued to practice and learn the many skills of fencing, she would be able to compete against anyone.

Although Sharon was one of only two girls who came out for the team and she had never known anything about fencing, she soon felt that this was where she belonged. In the musty room with the piled-up old wrestling mats, she had discovered her real home.

Sharon didn't care that the uniform she was given didn't seem to fit. The jacket was much too big and the sleeves a little too short. The stiff, thick cotton material — once white, but now a dull gray from years of use — was not very comfortable. She got used to the stale odor. It smelled like it had been in a closet too long.

Yet, as Sharon's fingers worked the silver buttons on the jacket that covered her neck and closed the velcro on her baggy pants, called breeches, she felt a real sense of pride. One of her new teammates

helped her with the zipper in back. She adjusted the strap that went from the front of the jacket, through her legs, and buckled in back.

Sharon would carefully attach the protective metal vest over her fencing jacket and fit on the mesh mask which shielded her face.

The big, padded leather glove seemed to swallow her hand. The protective gauntlet covered her arm up to her elbow.

She stood tall as she grasped the delicate looking sword. The image that looked back at her from the practice mirror no longer resembled that of the gawky youngster, too shy to look a classmate in the face. The girl in the mirror moved gracefully with an air of real confidence.

Sharon was usually the last one to leave practice in the afternoon. Over and over she would repeat the exercises that the coach had given her. The complicated foot movements — the swift hard lunges, the nimble parries to avoid her opponent's attack — came to her quickly and naturally.

Sharon had grown strong and powerful. She loved the quick, non-stop action during training. She loved the hard work and the sense of accomplishment that her workouts gave her. But she especially enjoyed the looks of respect she saw in the eyes of her teammates.

One day during a short rest break, Sharon told Mr. Fine that sometimes she imagined there was an eye at the tip of her foil. The eye saw chances to score points with a quick touch to her opponent's torso even before her own eyes behind the mask. Coach Fine said nothing. He nodded and then he smiled. Sharon knew that she was on the right track.

She soon became part of the six-person Roosevelt Fencing Team, which traveled to compete against other high school teams throughout the New York City area — in the Bronx and in Manhattan and in Queens as well. There were two "A" competitors, two "B" competitors, and two "C" competitors. That first year, Sharon usually competed as a B-fencer, which meant that she often was matched against one of the better fencers from a competing school. Of course, the better Sharon got, the better her opponents seemed to become.

Almost always she fenced against a boy, and that was OK with Sharon. It wasn't always OK with the boys, though. As the season moved along, she found that she won more than she lost. If the others were teased about losing to a girl, well, that was just something they would have to learn to deal with!

Now that Sheila had left home, Sharon spent more and more time in the practice room and less time in her cold apartment. Each week, Sharon got better and better at fencing. She began to think of herself as a real athlete. It was funny. Everyone seemed proud of Sharon's success — everyone, that is, except her mom.

Sharon tried to explain what fencing meant to her, but her mom didn't understand why being a fencer was so important to Sharon. Her mom did not seem to know how to give Sharon any encouragement. Coach Fine and the members of the team were the "family" that made her feel good.

• • •

In the spring, it was time for the Public School League Individual Championships in Fencing. Sharon was chosen as one of the members of the Roosevelt High School Team at the big tournament. During the subway ride out to the competition, Sharon's stomach began to feel funny. By the time she had dressed for the bout and walked out on the gymnasium floor, the feeling had spread down her arms to her fingers. The foil, usually a natural part of her arm, seemed clumsy in her hand. The competition room was big and noisy. Sharon felt small and quiet.

The bout had just started, and Sharon was already two hits behind. Her feet were stuck to the floor. Her body had double-crossed her. Where was the parry that she had been practicing every day? Instead of speedy and limber, she was slow and stiff. The self-confidence that Coach Fine always said was so necessary in a good fencer drained from her body like rain water down a spout.

What was wrong? All those hours of practice and

hard work, and now she couldn't remember what to do. What happened to her counterattack? Her opponent moved swiftly and gracefully, hitting his target dead-on. The point of his foil touched her torso. Just that fast she was out of the competition. She had let down her school and let down her team. Could she ever look Mr. Fine in the eyes again?

Suddenly, from nowhere an ugly shout escaped from Sharon's lips. She threw her mask down hard and watched in horror as it bounced against the polished wood floor and came to rest at the feet of Mr. Fine. The room began to spin out of control. The faces all around her — the spectators in the bleachers and her teammates — began to blur.

Now, embarrassed, Sharon tried hard to hold back the tears. She yanked off her glove and threw it behind her as she hurried into the locker room. Sitting on the bench, staring down at her feet, Sharon felt very sorry for herself. She felt very, very alone. As she stood up, she spotted her reflection in the locker room mirror. She did not like what she saw. Sharon learned something important that day. She hated to lose.

3

Right of Way

It was early on a biting cold Saturday morning in late March. The number six train rumbled and shook its way toward Manhattan. Sharon had folded herself into a corner seat of the half-empty subway car. She closed her eyes and remembered the argument she had that morning with her mother. It was an argument which never seemed to end. Sharon had jumped up from her half-eaten breakfast. She slammed the door and, not wanting to wait for the noisy old elevator, she stomped down the several flights of stairs. Always arguing about the money! Why couldn't her mom understand how important getting to fencing practice was to her? Didn't Mom know that fencing competition had become her whole life?

Sharon's determination on Mr. Fine's team had gotten her an invitation to join the weekend practices at the New York Fencer's Club, which was downtown at 38th and Madison. Every Saturday Sharon and her mom had the same old disagreement. They would argue about the cost of the two tokens for the subway! It took one token to get downtown to the fencing club for training and one token to get home.

If her mom would really listen to Sharon, she would hear the joy in her voice when she talked about fencing. Mom might begin to understand how good Sharon felt as an athlete. So much of Sharon's life was out of her control. Being poor and growing up in the South Bronx meant she had fewer choices. And most of the important decisions about her life were made by her mom, anyway.

On the fencing mat it was different. This was where her very own decisions counted. She could decide what move to make, and she could lose a point or win the whole thing! It was a very powerful feeling.

● ● ●

Sharon trudged through the tired and dirty streets toward the subway. She dug her hands deeply into her pockets and steadied her shoulders against the cold wind. Her cold weather jacket, which had belonged to Sheila, was now much too small for her. She had grown taller, but she no longer felt awkward about it. She had also grown stronger from all the physical training and practice for her sport.

She walked past shells of abandoned buildings. Smoke stained the bricks around the broken windows. She passed block after block of empty lots,

littered with piles of rubbish and beer bottles. In her imagination, the solitary buildings became people — old, broken and alone — staring outward with blind eyes.

It was hard for Sharon to explain to her mom how she usually felt. Because of her unsafe neighborhood and poor apartment, everyday Sharon risked her health and safety. Most of her life, Sharon felt stuck in a troubled world. Fencing was a way to get unstuck!

If her mom really looked, she could see in Sharon's eyes the thrill and excitement when she thought about beginning to compete. There was that wonderful moment of waiting to get onto the mat. It was like a million butterflies in her stomach, but she loved that feeling. What could she do so that her mom could feel the excitement, too? How could she make her mom truly understand how really happy being a competitive fencer made Sharon feel?

● ● ●

Still daydreaming about the fight with her mom, Sharon opened her eyes with a quick start as the subway pulled into the 86th Street stop. A tall young man with long hair and a dark beard boarded the car traveling down toward the city. He carried a large case with a musical instrument. "He's probably taking lessons down at Julliard College," she thought. A woman who wore a black coat over a black dress carried a large portfolio of drawings. Sharon wondered, "Was she learning to be a famous artist, heading all the way down to Greenwich Village?" There was a lot going on in this exciting new world. Sharon wanted very much to be part of it.

At 59th Street a beautiful woman got on, holding tightly to the hands of two little girls. The older girl wore a blue ballerina dress under her warm wool coat. She looked just like her mom. They both had lovely, thick, dark hair pulled back in a bun. Her little sister looked so cute. She wore a pink ballerina's dress. In her short hair she had a pink headband with a pink rose at the top. Her coat matched her big sister's.

Both girls carried their satin dancing shoes by their ribbon ties. They whispered to each other and giggled excitedly. Sharon stood up and began inching her way to the door in the middle of the train. The car had filled up with busy people on a Saturday morning in New York.

Sharon climbed the steps up from the subway platform at 33rd Street and Park Avenue. The bright sun helped ease the early spring chill. Its light reflected back and forth from a thousand sheets of glass on the tall office buildings. The sidewalk became a checkerboard of bright squares and dark shadows. This really was a magical world, a place where anything could happen.

• • •

As Sharon crossed the street to head west toward Madison Avenue, she noticed how much cleaner the streets were in this part of the city. She counted the blocks from 33rd to 38th Street. She always counted these few blocks. She was so eager to get there. Sharon entered the Hotel Lancaster and took the elevator to the third floor.

The first time Sharon came to the New York Fencer's Club, she thought it was funny that they rented a floor in a hotel. Mr. Fine had encouraged Sharon to go when she got the invitation from Eric Rosenberg to join. It was a free fencing program for kids every Saturday morning from 9 a.m. to noon. There were about 30 young fencers training from ages 10 to 17 there.

Mr. Fine had said that joining this special program was an honor. It was how Sharon would go from being good to being great. She could really learn much more from Eric Rosenberg than Mr. Fine could teach her.

"I like fencing at school," Sharon said. "I feel comfortable with my teammates, here. I don't know if I want to go all the way into Manhattan and compete against kids better than me."

Mr. Fine could see that Sharon was a little afraid. He tried to ease her worry. "Sharon, fencing is fencing. You'll be practicing the same exercise routines as you do at school."

"But..."

"You're ready. You're ready for the next level. And Eric Rosenberg will help you get there."

Maybe the fencing was the same thing, but the gym of the New York Fencer's Club sure was different. There were clean white walls with nice lockers. And there was no musty smell! There was even a nice shower area. And the fencing uniforms were a lot cleaner - they even looked white, not dirty gray. The equipment was newer and in much better condition than at Roosevelt High School. Eric Rosenberg used more modern scoring machines for their training and matches.

When Sharon first saw Eric Rosenberg, she immediately noticed that he had big glasses just like her, and he slouched a little just like her. She also knew right away that he was a very good teacher. He did not yell at any of the kids.

And Eric noticed some things instantly about Sharon, too. He could see right from the beginning that Sharon had a tremendous physical ability to be a great fencer one day. She was tall with long arms and legs. And her legs were very, very strong. He could tell some other things about Sharon, too. She had a lot of energy, and she was very eager to learn more about fencing.

One of the early memories Eric has of Sharon is of the first words she said to him, "I am ready to work." He thought that this was very unusual for a young woman to say. She was a hard worker in the fencing gym. She would practice again and again to get a new skill right.

She had very little patience for making mistakes. Eric could also see a lot of anger in the way Sharon reacted to losing points. It sometimes made it difficult to deal with her. He knew that this was one of the first skills that he had to work on with Sharon.

Sharon, however, was more interested in learning the great footwork that Eric Rosenberg was famous for. He had been a college fencer himself, and he loved the sport. She wanted Eric to teach her everything he knew so that she could do her very best.

• • •

It was another Saturday morning at the Fencing Club. The fencers were told to take their positions on the fencing surface — a long mat called a piste. The piste is about 45 feet long and about 6 and half feet wide. It is marked by a center line and by en garde lines to show where the fencers stand to begin the match. There are also warning lines and lines to mark the back limit. When the athlete is fencing, he or she must stay within these lines.

In foil competition, scoring is done electronically. Eric showed the fencers how a wire connects the piste to red and green lights. The wire passes under the fencer's jacket and attaches to the hilt, or handle, of the sword. When the tip of the fencer's foil touches the opponent's metal vest, the electrical circuit is completed. A light flashes — red for one fencer, green for the other — showing that a point has been scored. That is how the judges know who has scored the point.

Sharon already knew that the rules of fencing were a little complicated. Points can only be scored when a fencer is on the attack. This means that the fencer must make a thrust by fully extending the weapon arm before the opponent has a chance. The other fencer must first parry, or block, the blade of the attacker's sword. When the fencer does this, he or she is allowed to riposte, or go on the attack. The first attacker, in turn, tries to parry and attack again.

The lesson was clear. "The bout is won," Eric always liked to say, "not on the mat, but between the ears. Strategy is most important. Fencing is a high speed game of chess." Eric spent a lot of time teaching about strategy or the plan of action that a fencer takes.

Attack. Parry. Counterattack. Sharon practiced hour after hour. Soon, she was able to see the match in her mind's eye even before it had actually begun. She saw her opening move. She anticipated what her opponent's move would be. She could imagine what move she would make next to score a hit. Sharon was learning all about strategy.

● ● ●

Still, Sharon could not forget her bitter loss at the last public league championships and how miserable she had felt. She remembered the tight feeling in her throat. It felt as though she had forgotten how to breathe.

"Make the nervousness work for you," explained Eric, "to give you a competitive edge over your opponents. Don't let it paralyze you and make your body freeze. When you start to get nervous, you want to use that energy and make sure you keep moving and breathing." Eric emphasized, "Breathing is very important." This thought made Sharon laugh out loud.

"You are giggling because you think that you know how to breathe — just because you do it all the time. But there are special ways to breathe that can help you to relax and concentrate and make you a better fencer." Then Eric proved it to her. He had Sharon feel her own heartbeat as she breathed in her normal quick, nervous way. She counted out the heartbeats for 10 seconds. Then he taught her how to breathe for fencing.

"Breathe in deeply through your nose. Let the air fill up first from your belly and then up to the top of your chest. Then let it out slowly through your mouth. Now try it again, only this time imagine that the air is a stream of purple smoke that you can see going in your nose, filling up your chest, and out through your mouth.

"Inhale again, and this time, when you let out the air, I want to hear you sigh." Sharon was puzzled.

"What do you mean?" she asked.

"I mean that I want to hear a noise coming out of you as you let the air go, something like 'ahhhh' or 'whuuuu.'" After Sharon practiced picturing the colorful air and sighing with each exhale, Eric asked her to again count her heartbeats with her special breathing method. Sharon was amazed at the effect the new breathing was having. There were fewer heartbeats in the 10 second time period, and she definitely felt calmer.

Eric continued, "It is important to be calm, because it helps you to think clearly. When we get nervous, our thoughts get jumbled, and we get confused. But a good fencer needs to be sharp-minded every minute. Another way to do this is to gently get rid of the nervous tension in your body before you fence."

Eric demonstrated while giving Sharon instructions. "Bend your knees and let your head and shoulders slump forward. Let your whole body become a wet noodle. Now shake that tension out from your neck, down through your arms, and right out your fingers." Sharon did it too.

Sharon wondered, "When should I do these things to calm down? Should I do the breathing and the shaking out the tension the night before a competition or when I get to the gym? Because I am usually pretty calm in my matches."

Eric frowned and lowered his voice, "How about those famous temper tantrums of yours?" Sharon was embarrassed. She swallowed hard and looked down at the floor. When she looked up she saw that Eric was smiling. He really wasn't upset at all. Sharon smiled too. Soon, they were both laughing together. Sharon and Eric would go on to become lifelong friends.

"In all seriousness, your temper does get in your way. For one thing it can zap you of your energy and make you too tired to enjoy fencing. You must allow yourself to really enjoy your sport. What do you do when you get mad about losing a point?" he asked Sharon.

"I sometimes throw my mask." she answered, "I am sorry about that."

"Sorry isn't the point, Sharon. What could you do instead of throwing your mask?"

Sharon thought a moment and happily answered, "I could do some deep breathing and sighing, or shake out like a wet noodle!"

"That's right!" Eric said. "Fencing is a blast. You should be having fun. Competition is what makes it fun and exciting. Winning and losing are part of competition."

Sharon was learning that keeping calm under pressure was a most important part of becoming a top athlete. Eric continued, "A fencer is like an artist — a person who does something with extraordinary skill. The joy is in the performance and in making the performance joyful. The winning will follow."

She was learning the art of fencing from Eric. He was teaching her the musical rhythm, the dance steps, the perfect body positions. At that moment, Sharon realized how much she was like the artist, the musician and the ballerinas on the subway. She too was learning to create something beautiful.

● ● ●

The hours flew by. Fencing was fun! Sharon loved fencing, and she loved hanging out with Eric and the other fencers. But she hated when it was time to go home.

Sharon walked out the door of the Hotel Lancaster. The bright morning sun had almost disappeared. A thin light was showing through the pale, flat, gray skies. It had grown even colder. Sharon walked and walked in no special hurry to get home. The wind from the East River had picked up and brought with it the threat of an early spring snow storm.

On the next corner a man sold warm roasted nuts from a cart with a green and white umbrella. Sharon loved the smell. She was cold and she was hungry. She felt in her pocket for coins. Her mom had given her exactly enough money to take the subway into Manhattan and back uptown again. Mom was always ready to remind her that they had better uses for the money, too. Sharon quickly stepped down into the subway and headed home.

● ● ●

During the next year Sharon started to dream about going to college and being on a college fencing team. A few months later a large white envelope arrived. Sharon Monplaisir had been accepted at the University of Wisconsin. She had earned a full scholarship. Sharon was thrilled. She would be able to work toward her college degree, and she would be able to continue fencing.

Sharon skipped excitedly outside into the gentle rain. She turned up her head and let the drops wash over her face. In a corner of the vacant lot next to her building a flower had started growing between all the trash and broken glass. A beautiful blossom had opened, a few drops of spring rain clinging to its petals.

4

Scoring Points

Sharon lay curled up in the back of the old van. Her head rested uncomfortably on a rolled-up sweat shirt that she used as a pillow. She tried to manage a few hours of sleep, but with the constant banging and grinding of the old engine as the van climbed the foothills of the Rocky Mountains, sleep did not come easily.

Sharon had become one of the top female fencers at the University of Wisconsin. Along with a few of her teammates, she had been chosen to compete at the U.S. National Championships held in Colorado Springs, Colorado. A fellow student on the Wisconsin men's team was making the trip in a rusty old van and Sharon had saved up just enough to chip in her share of the gas money. Trying to stretch a few dollars a long way, Sharon lived on hot dogs, cold beans from a can, and containers of hot coffee. She was so excited to be competing in her first national championship, that Sharon forgot how tired and hungry she really was.

Most of the competitors had their own uniforms

made just for them. They had their own foil weapons along with them, too. Their foils had specially made grips and had been balanced just the way they liked them. Sharon had borrowed an old uniform from the equipment room at the University. She had had to borrow two foils from Eric Rosenberg, but only one was really working properly.

Sharon would stay at the Olympic Training Center during the tournament. This was a very exciting place to be. Sharon knew that many famous Olympic athletes from many sports trained and competed here. This was where the best in the world came to learn about the newest training techniques from the finest coaches and exercise scientists. The athletes wanted to get stronger and faster and sharper for their sport. Some had been selected for the Olympic team based on their performance here, and some had gone home having missed their chance for a dream. It was a great place for world-class athletes to come together.

But it was not world-class housing. The Olympic Training Center was where an old Air Force base used to be. The fencers slept four to a room on narrow bunks with thin mattresses. Each athlete was given two small towels, a set of sheets, a single blanket and a pillow. Everyone ate in a community dining hall in a nearby building. There were no radios or T.V.s in the room. But to Sharon, it was like staying in the fanciest hotel on 5th Avenue. The night before the tournament Sharon felt calm and happy. In fact, she was the happiest she had ever been.

• • •

The championship started at 8 o'clock the next morning and would last all day. Almost 100 female fencers — the best in the country — would be competing for the title of U.S. National Champion. The competition was open to girls and women of all ages. They had all worked for years to earn the chance to fence at this tournament. There was a lot of pressure. Everyone wanted to win.

The gym was a huge room with a polished wood floor. Folding chairs were scattered about here and there for the athletes waiting to fence, waiting for the signal "En Garde." Rows of fluorescent lights on the high ceiling cast a strange glow over the room. A long banner was taped along one wall:

1979 U.S. NATIONAL FENCING CHAMPIONSHIPS

Sharon Monplaisir, not yet 18 years old, was about to take her place among the finest amateur, or non-professional, athletes in the world. Sharon watched the other women go through their warm-up exercises. This was the routine that they did before a competition to get their bodies and minds ready for action. They were good. Some were very good. On the other side of the gym, Sharon saw Gay D'Saro practicing with another fencer.

47

1979 US NATIONAL FENCING CHAMPIONSHIP

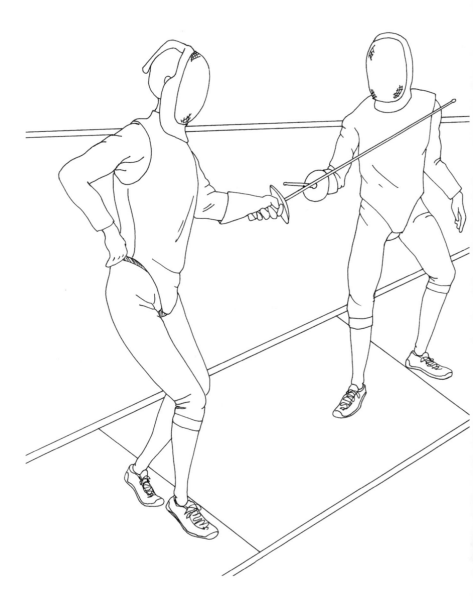

Gay was well-known as one of the best fencers in the country. Sharon studied her every move. She was quick, and she was graceful. Her footwork was perfect. It was like watching a great ballerina glide across the floor — only much, much faster. Her practice partner could not keep up with Gay's moves. In the blink of an eye, Sharon saw Gay thrust her sword and make her hit. So, this was what the sport of fencing was all about.

Sharon should have been panicking. She remembered her attack of nerves before her first high school championships. She thought about how her nervousness had caused her to lose her concentration and then lose the bout. Now, looking around the room at all these amazing competitors, Sharon started to get herself ready the way Eric Rosenberg had taught her. All she had to do was her same routine — as if she were back at the fencing club.

She thought about the countless hours of practice at the New York Fencer's Club. Sharon recalled all the footwork exercises, the parrying strategies, and the endless exercise routines. Sharon laughed to herself as she remembered Eric's advice, "Don't forget to breathe." So Sharon began her relaxing routine to settle herself down.

She took a long, slow breath in through her nose. She imagined a colorful stream of air filling up her body from the bottom up to the top of her chest. She let the breath slowly out through her mouth. She repeated this four times, and by the fourth time she felt steady and calm. Next she did her wet noodle routine. Sharon shook out the stiffness from her neck and shoulders, shook out her arms — all the way to her fingertips. Sharon was ready.

A sense of excitement pulsed through her veins. It was a great feeling. Sharon was thrilled. Here on the gym floor, among her fellow fencers from so many backgrounds all over the United States, Sharon felt that this was where she belonged.

The tournament was about to begin. Fencers crossed the room to form pools of six competitors. The top three winners of each pool would advance to the next round. This would continue all day until only six fencers were left in the final round. Gay D'Saro walked by Sharon. She stopped a moment and gave her a big smile and a few words of friendly encouragement.

"En-Garde!" the official called out. The fencers got into the ready position. He then called, "Allez." The match had begun. Sharon moved quickly through the early rounds. She was fencing with an easy confidence. Hour after hour passed. Sharon was in terrific condition, and she seemed to grow stronger and faster as she continued to win. She moved forward from one round to the next. Her tactics worked. She could imagine her possible plan of attack two and three moves ahead of time. In her mind's eye the action seemed to get slower and slower, just as the footwork and sword play of the match quickened.

Sharon had heard that these tournaments could last 10 to 12 hours. It was a long time to be paying attention. It was the middle of June in Colorado, but there was no way for Sharon to know what it was like outside. There were no windows in this large gym. All she saw, hour after hour, were fencers fencing or fencers sitting around waiting for their next bout.

There was some time before her next contest. Sharon sat in one of the stacking chairs that were scattered near the fencing strips. She looked around the room. Most of the fencers had fancy outfits and four or five weapons to choose from. She also began to think about how hungry she was. She was letting her mind wander, and she was getting a little distracted. It was time to concentrate on what she had to do — she had to focus on only herself. There was a trick that she had learned to make herself pay attention.

Sharon rested her hands on her knees. She closed her eyes gently. She tried to stay very still. She did not move a muscle. She had to really concentrate to do this. Then, when she was very still, Sharon imagined blue skies with big fluffy clouds. She put all her thoughts about the other competitors and the judges and the scores and especially of being hungry — on the clouds. She loaded up the clouds with these thoughts. Then she just let them float away.

Then Sharon brought her imagination back to how still her body was and how each part of her body felt sitting in the chair. She thought about her calm breathing. She stood up and tried to balance her arms out from her sides. She felt in perfect balance. Then she slowly opened her eyes. She did not even notice all the activity around her. Sharon was ready once again.

• • •

Sharon took her position on the fencing strip. She scored one quick hit, then another. Suddenly disaster struck! Sharon's only working weapon was broken. Fencers in tournament play are responsible for their own equipment. If Sharon did not have a working foil, she would be out of the competition. She felt a tug on her arm. Sharon turned to find Gay offering one of her own foils for Sharon to use. Sharon was so thankful. It was such a generous thing for Gay to do. This was real sportsmanship. It was so unselfish to help out an opponent in the middle of the tournament.

There was only one problem. Gay was right-handed. Sharon was left-handed. The grip on the foil was backward. It felt awkward in Sharon's hand. It was difficult to hold the foil, but Sharon did not care. She just wanted to compete. Sharon was not about to let this or anything else interfere with her chance for success.

It turned out that later in the day, Sharon had to compete against Gay with the weapon Gay had let her borrow. The action was very, very fast. Sharon was moving very well. She was using all the best routines that Eric had taught her and which she had practiced and practiced in college. Now, however, something new was happening. In the heat of the competition, Sharon stopped thinking about which routine would work best and began to just let the action flow. Sharon was fencing better than she had ever fenced in her life. She beat Gay by an unusually good score of five touches to one.

The two women, both fierce competitors, hugged after the bout. It was the strange combination of feelings that good competitors have for each other. Both fencers had wanted to win with all their heart. Each respected the skills and effort of the other. Sharon and Gay felt both warmth and rivalry for each other. And of course, they both had love and respect for the challenge of the sport of fencing, too.

Although Sharon was one of the youngest athletes competing, and although she had been fencing for only a few years, she finished in the top 20 of the National Championships.

This was a great achievement. She was very proud and felt good about who she had become.

Sharon couldn't wait to phone Eric and tell him about her success. She knew that he had played an important part. She told Eric about each and every move in the bout. He could hear the excitement in her voice.

Of course, there was now one other problem as well. Sharon had spent what little money she had getting from the University of Wisconsin to Colorado Springs. She had almost nothing left to get back again. The only thing she could think of to do was to hitchhike a ride from a stranger. Well, getting back to school would be an adventure. But, to tell the truth, it wasn't exactly an adventure she was looking forward to.

● ● ●

The next day found Sharon, backpack over her shoulder, with her thumb out on the highway out of town. The skies were endless and blue with only a few wispy white clouds high above. To the west the jagged snow-capped Rocky Mountains stretched as far as the eye could see. To the east the blacktop road went on forever and ever. Sharon let the warm sunshine wash down upon her upturned face and daydreamed a bit.

She thought of mom and Sheila thousands of miles away. She remembered sharing her dreams with them so many years ago. Sharon smiled thinking of Coach Fine and those first days of practice with George and her other teammates in the Roosevelt fencing gym.

"Was that only two years ago?" she asked herself.

"Yes, two years and a whole lifetime." And, of course, Sharon recalled with a smile of quiet satisfaction the Saturday mornings at the fencing club with her good friend Eric.

Suddenly, an old pickup truck pulled along side Sharon. She could see that there were three guys in it. The driver offered Sharon a ride. He seemed friendly enough, but there was something in his voice that made Sharon a little uncomfortable. She thought about the lessons she had learned as a young girl in the South Bronx. She had learned who she could trust and who she couldn't trust. Sharon had learned to believe in herself and trust her instincts.

Sharon turned down the offer of the ride. But the men in the truck would not leave. She started to run back toward town. The driver threw the pick-up truck into reverse and followed her down the highway. The men became nasty and shouted at her. Sharon had always been able to take care of herself, but now she became terribly frightened. Just then another car pulled up. The driver seemed to understand the danger. He opened the passenger door and Sharon quickly jumped in. She let out a deep sigh of relief. Her heart was pounding furiously.

"Maybe that's something else fencing has taught me," she told herself sadly. "Never let your guard down."

● ● ●

Sometime later, Sharon was dropped off in a small town outside Omaha, Nebraska. She was still shaken from the creepy people in the pickup truck. Sharon knew she had to look for help. She went to a church and explained her problem to the pastor. He was a nice man and he wanted to help. He offered her some tea as he patiently listened to Sharon's story. His face grew troubled and sad when Sharon told him about the scary three men. He pinched the bridge of his nose and picked up the phone to make a few calls.

He persuaded an older woman who belonged to the church to loan Sharon enough money for a bus ride back to school in Wisconsin. Sharon promised to pay back the money. And she did — every penny, although it took her almost a year.

Sharon had gone out to discover the world. She had tried her best, and she had done very well. Somewhere along the way a young girl who had been given very few advantages in life had become a proud and successful woman.

5

Making a Hit

"Quiet! Quiet, please. Boys and girls may I have your attention?" Mr. Tartaglia, the middle-school principal, stood on the stage behind the podium and shouted into the microphone. Although it was very cold outside on this February morning, here in the old school auditorium it was quite warm. The principal wiped some beads of sweat from his shiny, bald head.

Some of the boys in Mr. Hartwig's class were laughing loudly and making rude noises. Mrs. Lessing, the gym teacher, was hushing some of the giggling girls in her home room class. Others kids were whispering excitedly about something that had happened in the hall before assembly. One girl, with glasses sliding down her nose, sat all by herself on the very last row and seemed to be studying her shoes with great seriousness. No one seemed to be paying attention to poor Mr. Tartaglia.

"Students, please. Today we have a very special guest." Mr. Tartaglia stood on his tiptoes and shouted even louder into the microphone. A horrible screeching sound came from the speakers on both sides of the auditorium stage. The boys and girls laughed even louder and began to hold their ears to muffle the noise.

Mr. Tartaglia backed up a step. "Boys and girls, what do you get when you combine the reflexes of a boxer, the legs of a high-jumper, and the concentration of a chess player? How about a champion fencer? Today, we have a very special guest. Miss Monplaisir is a three-time Olympic athlete. Her sport is fencing. Today, she is here from the Women's Sports Foundation to help us celebrate National Girls and Women in Sports Day."

Gradually the students stopped laughing and whispering and making silly noises. Everyone turned to look at the young woman who sat tall and straight in a chair at the side of the stage. The children and teachers wanted to know more about this person who had come to visit their school. She was wearing a pretty, black suit with a short skirt. She had a very close-cropped haircut, and her beautiful face glowed when she smiled at the mention of her name.

Mr. Tartaglia continued in a quieter voice. "Miss Monplaisir is a four-time NCAA All-American Fencer, first at the University of Wisconsin, and then, at Hunter College, here in New York. She competed as a member of the World University Team in 1983, and again in 1987. She was a member of the U.S.

World Fencing Team from 1985 to 1991. Miss Monplaisir was on the gold medal winning team that competed in the Pan-American Games in 1987 and again in 1991. She was the 1988 U.S. National Champion."

Mr. Tartaglia paused to clear his throat. Now, he had everyone's complete attention. The only sound in the room was the clanging and hissing of the steam pipes in the back of the auditorium.

"Miss Monplaisir competed as a member of the United States Olympic team in three different Olympic Games in three different countries on three different continents. This is a fantastic accomplishment attained by only a very small number of athletes."

A loud burst of applause followed Mr. Tartaglia's introduction. Many of the kids and even some of the teachers stood to show their respect for this world-class athlete and her many achievements.

And when she stood to walk over to the microphone, her black high heels made her look even taller than imagined. What the students saw was a strikingly beautiful woman with long, long legs. She crossed the stage in a few easy, graceful steps. She was a confident and strong female athlete. They could tell just by the way she moved that this was someone special. She had a wonderful smile which seemed to light up the room on this dull winter's day in February.

Everyone's eyes were on her as she took a moment

to adjust the microphone. The boys and girls paid careful attention and were waiting expectantly. Only the little girl on the end of the very last row continued to stare down at her shoes.

Sharon began to speak. "Thank you for the kind introduction. Each time I hear those words, even I am amazed. Especially because I know what a wonderful journey it has been. I learned how to fence in high school. I attended college on an athletic scholarship and became an Olympic fencer, competing around the world.

"Even after all those years of hard work, training and competitions, I never really felt like a great athlete until the opening ceremonies of the Los Angeles Olympics in 1984. The Olympics are international competitions of the world's best athletes and are held every four years in a different country. The event in 1984 was extra special because it took place in my own country. There were over 7,000 athletes from all over the world, and 100,000 spectators in the stadium and millions watching on T.V."

"Everywhere you looked in the stadium, you could see the flags with the Olympic symbol — five connected rings of blue, black, red, yellow and green. These rings represent the continents of Africa, North and South America, Asia, Australia, and Europe. The athletes from all the other countries marched in perfectly straight rows. But the U.S. athletes were so excited that we forgot all about marching and swarmed into the stadium — running and jumping and shouting. Everyone was so happy and so excited and so very proud to be representing our country. We all took pictures of one another and showed off our wonderful uniforms. It was so cool.

"I stood on the playing field of the Coliseum in Los Angeles. Thousands of brightly colored streamers swirled in the air. Fireworks lit up the sky. I watched in amazement as Rafer Johnson, the great American decathlon gold-medal winner, ran all the way up the steps with the Olympic torch. He then lit the big flame on top of the stadium that signaled the start of the Olympic Games. I knew I would always remember that feeling and that special moment."

The boys and girls sat perfectly still in their seats listening to Miss Monplaisir. Their eyes were wide with anticipation. Mr. Tartaglia was sitting on the edge of his seat, and he had a great big smile on his face.

"On the day of my first Olympic fencing competition, I remember seeing many of my friends sitting among the spectators. They were there to cheer for me and my teammates on the United States Fencing Team. It was a wonderful moment for me. When I had a break between team events, I would go into the stands with my friends. Little kids and big kids and dads and moms, too, all came over to ask for my autograph and say a few words of encouragement."

"The U.S. team was not the best in the world, and everyone knew it. And there was not much of a chance for me to win a gold medal. But all of these people were really proud of me just because I was an Olympian — an Olympian who was part of their country. Friends and strangers were proud of me for all the work I did to get there. I was representing the United States regardless of whether or not I had a medal. All these people in the stands in Los Angeles gave me something very special — they gave me encouragement and support, no matter what the outcome of my event.

"Because of them, I finally realized that it was OK to be proud of myself. Also, for the first time in my life, I understood that competing was even more important than winning."

Miss Monplaisir pretended to get very serious. She shook her finger at all of the students and teachers sitting in the auditorium.

"But don't think for a single moment that I didn't want to win!" She was kidding, but she was serious, too.

"In 1988, I made the U.S. Olympic team for the second time, and this time we all got to travel to a land very far from home. The 1988 Olympic Games were held in Seoul, Korea. S - E - O - U - L, which is pronounced like "soul" music or the "sole" of your shoe. It is the capital and largest city in South Korea. It is in Asia, not far from China. It is about as far as a girl from New York City could possibly go!

"Seoul is a city of great differences. There are Buddhist temples and royal palaces more than a thousand years old. But there are also modern high rise apartment buildings and shiny new department stores as magnificent as any you might see in the United States. Just like the city and the buildings, the people can be very much like Americans, and they can be very different.

"For example, in many Korean restaurants the floors are covered with straw mats, and it is considered good manners to remove your shoes before entering. Visitors are given flip-flops or slippers to wear instead. It is a little strange to see a pile of shoes by the doorway of a restaurant."

One of the boys in the audience pinched his nose between his thumb and finger and shouted, "Pee-yew!" The other boys and girls started to laugh. Mr. Tartaglia had an angry look on his face. He turned to the guest speaker, but she too was laughing along with everyone else.

"It is a custom in Korea for people to exchange small gifts. It has also become a tradition for athletes from different countries to trade gifts at the Olympic Games. They trade sweat bands, T-shirts, warm-ups and small pins with their countries' colors and flags. Even the athletes from countries that are not friends with the United States love to trade for anything with the red, white and blue USA letters. Some people get very serious about collecting stuff, but, mostly it is a way to meet and talk with participants from all over the world.

"In 1992, I made my third Olympic fencing team, and I had a feeling that this just might be my last. I made up my mind to enjoy this great experience and to treasure every special moment. The games were held in Barcelona, a city in Spain on the Mediterranean Sea. A Spanish archer opened the Games by shooting a fiery arrow, lit by the Olympic Torch, to light the flame on top of the Olympic Stadium of Montjuic. It was a magical moment.

"And Barcelona is a magical city. Tall, pointy towers reach to the sky. Many buildings are decorated with colorful tiles and bits of glass that reflect the rays of sunlight. It is a little like a real-life Disneyland. And it is a town that does not sleep. When my competition was over, I did get a chance to go out with some friends and do a little dancing. People there don't eat dinner until 10 o'clock at night, and many of the clubs open at midnight. The music and the dancing go on till 4 or 5 in the morning.

"There were over 10,000 athletes from 171 different countries in Barcelona. It was also very special because it was the first time in 32 years that athletes from the country of South Africa were allowed to compete in the Olympics.

"South Africa had finally stopped apartheid — where people of color and white people were not allowed to live and work and go to school together. When South Africa gave people of color more rights, they were invited back into the Games. So it was a time of new hope during the 16 days and nights of the Barcelona Olympics.

"I remember one night I came into the cafeteria late because I had stopped off at the training gym for a short workout. It was after my team had already eaten. I looked around the room, and there weren't many familiar faces, and most of the seats were taken. One athlete from another country motioned for me to join him and his teammates. I noticed that they all had thick necks and huge shoulders and chests. But they all had friendly smiles, too. They were the Bulgarian weight-lifting team. Now, I don't speak any Bulgarian, and they knew very little English, but the next two hours were spent laughing and talking with our hands and using little bits of different languages.

"It's funny, but for me, even more than the ceremonies and the competitions, it was moments like those in the cafeteria that showed the true spirit of the Games. Young people, men and women, big and small, black and white and brown and yellow, from everywhere on earth got to know each other, not as Americans or Russians, but as people. And that's what I hope you will remember... how everyone can learn to get along with each other. Thank you for your attention today."

Everyone started cheering and raising their hands in frantic motion, trying to get Miss Monplaisir's attention. Mr. Tartaglia said, "We have time for a few questions. Who has a question? Please, raise your hand." He looked around at all the wiggling hands. "Yes, young lady in the blue sweater, stand and ask your question."

"My family comes from Korea. Do you remember anything special you saw there?"

"Yes, one day I went to a place to learn about the special ritual tea ceremony that they have. It was really interesting. They don't just pour the water and drink the tea. The whole ceremony can take a couple of hours. It is very spiritual. And the tea is green and foamy!

"Another thing I liked was attending an I-KE-BA-NA class. It was a flower arranging class. Their culture really believes in seeing the beauty around us, and enjoying the beauty of nature. One thing I remember the woman telling us was that every flower grows toward the sun — it is its positive side — and we have to find the positive side in everything."

She pointed to a young boy waving in the back, "Yes, next question."

"Is fencing like in Zorro or Star Wars?" the boy asked.

Miss Monplaisir turned and reached behind the table on the stage. She held up a foil weapon and a big mesh fencing mask. She put the mask on and held her weapon out and took her en garde position. The boys and girls watched with delight as she whipped the blade through the air, stepping forward and back, doing a lunge, and going back to her en garde position. "That's about it with heels on!" she shouted. She removed the mask and went back to the microphone. "Like Star Wars," she said. "It's pretty fast."

"Did you ever beat any guys?" another boy shouted, with a wise-guy smile on his face. There were a lot of "oooo's" from the kids in the audience.

"I'm glad you asked that. Especially because today is the day we celebrate female athletes. Many great women athletes before me have had to prove themselves, like Billie Jean King and Wilma Rudolph. A great athlete, male or female, has to be born with natural abilities. But just as important as these natural skills are desire and determination. And that means practicing every day—on the days when it is fun and especially on the days when you are tired and it is a struggle."

"What is very important, for every young athlete is having the opportunity to play the sport you love. Today, there are two and a half million girls playing sports. Both girls and boys can have the talent to play and the guts to be successful, and we have to support everyone in their goals to be an athlete." She paused, "Of course, I beat guys — lots of them, and they sometimes defeated me, too."

She pointed to a chubby little girl with her hand up about halfway. "Yes?" asked the guest speaker.

"I like to play sports and all..." the student stammered. "Only, some of the kids tease me and say that I don't look like any athlete they ever saw!" There was some muffled laughter around the room.

Miss Monplaisir looked straight into the young girl's face. "Let me tell you a true story about a little girl I knew named Sharon. She grew up in a very poor neighborhood not far from here in the South Bronx. She was always being picked on by other kids because she looked funny — she was skinny and gawky and wore giant glasses. The kids said that she looked like a bug. She was so poor she wore her big sister's hand-me-downs that were too small for her. She was lonely and did not have many friends."

Now, for the first time, that little girl with glasses who sat in the back row suddenly looked up. The speaker continued with her story.

"But Sharon learned to love sports and to love being an athlete. She made good friends on her sports team. People became proud of her so she trained and practiced. And she became one of the best athletes in the country."

The speaker continued, "I don't know what an athlete is supposed to look like. In the Olympic village, among the very best athletes in the whole wide world, I saw people of every size and shape. I saw

72

tiny gymnasts who could twist their bodies and fly through the air. And I saw some women who threw the heavy shotput who were very big and powerfully built. All of these women were terrific athletes."

Mr. Tartaglia took the microphone. "One more question, please. Yes, you," he said pointing to an enthusiastic hand waving at him. The young girl giggled and asked, "Do the Olympic athletes ever go out together, you know, like boyfriend and girlfriend?"

A big grin formed on the Olympic athlete's face, and she seemed a little embarrassed. "It does happen that people who are Olympic athletes date and fall in love. They have so much in common and can really understand all the time and hard work that training for the Olympics takes. As a matter of fact, my husband, Michael, is a three-time Olympian. He's that cute guy standing in the very back." Everyone turned at once and stared, and there were whispers and giggles.

"Sport has been such an important part of our lives, and we have both gained so much from being athletes."

Mr. Tartaglia was at the microphone again. "I want to thank Miss Monplaisir for being our special guest today and sharing her wonderful experiences. She has been a real inspiration for everyone here. Let's show her our appreciation boys and girls."

Everyone jumped to their feet and applauded. Just

then, the bell rang and the students began to file out of their seats, talking excitedly about the Olympic athlete.

As the guest speaker gathered her things and reached for her coat, she noticed the little girl from the last row quietly approaching. She seemed very shy.

"Miss Monplaisir," the girl began, "I was wondering... that young girl you told us about... the girl named Sharon, who everybody picked on and who had trouble making friends... "

The tall athlete bent down and put her arm around the young girl's shoulder. "Yes, sweetie," she said. "What is it?"

"I was just wondering... I mean... was that little girl... "

"Yes, dear," she said, reaching out to shake the young girl's hand.

"You can call me Sharon."

Highlights in Sharon Monplaisir's Athletic Career

- Named to the United States Olympic Fencing Team in 1984, 1988 & 1992
- United States National Champion in 1988
- Member of the United States World Team from 1985 to 1992
- Member of the Pan-American Gold Medal Team in 1987 & 1991
- Member of the World University Team in 1983 & 1987
- National Collegiate Athletic Association (NCAA) All-American in 1983, 1985, 1986 & 1987
- Recipient of the Women's Sports Foundation Travel & Training Fund Grant in 1990

• • •

Sharon maintains an active life as a businesswoman, a personal trainer, a fashion model and an athlete.

Sports Talk

To Parents, Teachers, and Coaches:

In this section you will see a discussion of some of the issues presented by Sharon's story as a young female athlete. We also share with you some information about the influence of sports participation on girls, and we have suggested some discussion questions for you.

We encourage you to talk about some of these topics with the young reader. Starting a dialogue and exchanging ideas can enhance this story for the soon-to-be athlete and make the sports experience more enjoyable for the young, accomplished athlete.

Body Image

Before Sharon took up fencing, she was embarrassed by her tall, skinny, "bug-like" body. It really upset her when the other kids teased her about how tall and scrawny she was. Youngsters become aware of being fat or thin at a very early age. Both boys and girls can have distorted self-images about what they should look like. A lot of that has to do with the images they see in magazines and on television.

Sharon felt awkward about how tall and skinny she was. Most girls think, incorrectly, that they are overweight.

Becoming an athlete really changed Sharon's image of her physical self. In training and competing for her sport, she learned how elegantly she could move her body, how fast she could be, and how strong every part of her body could become. Sharon points out in the story that there are many different female body shapes among the athletes in different sports.

Girls are generally more negative about their bodies than boys. Through sports, girls can learn to view their bodies in a positive way. Fencing really helped Sharon to have a strong and healthy body image.

Q: Think of different sports — gymnastics, shot-put, pole vault, weightlifting, figure skating. What would your body have to look like to do well in these sports? What part of your body do you like the best?

Competing Against the Boys

Often girls and boys are competing together on a sports team. One of the issues for young Sharon was the reactions of the boys she was competing against. For some girls, it may be a better decision to play in an all-girls league. In many cases, girls learn fundamental sports skills later than boys. They may feel sensitive about their lack of skills. For some girls, the friendships and social interaction are the best part of sports. They may feel less intimidated about taking risks on an all-girls team.

Other girls may find playing with and against the boys is a real advantage. A co-ed situation allows boys and girls to play at a higher level of competition. In teen years, boys are generally taller, heavier and stronger than girls. But in many sports this is not a major problem. In fencing, Sharon needed skill, agility and coordination to be successful. To have fair co-ed teams, young athletes should be grouped according to skill level and size, rather than sex.

Q: What sports are boys and girls both good at? What sports do you think women are better at? What sports do you think men are better at?

Temper Tantrums

One of the important tasks that Sharon was continually working on was learning patience and how to hold her temper when she lost a point or the bout. This is a significant lesson to learn not only in sports but also in life. Getting angry during a competition can be very tiring, and it is a waste of energy. It is like giving away free points to your competitor.

One of the best things about sports competition is learning how to lose and still feel good about yourself. Young athletes can think of failure as a challenge to learn something new, a way to improve one's skills, to get stronger and better for the next time. Fencing, like many sports, teaches you to wait patiently for the right moment. Learning how to re-lax and calm down is one of the best ways to stay focused on the contest.

Q: What did Sharon mean when she said, "Also, for the first time in my life, I understood that competing was even more important than winning"?

The Benefits of Sports Participation for Girls

More than ever before, American girls are actively involved in sports. Recent research has demon-strated the importance and value of exercise and sports for girls. These lessons learned in childhood help to shape the developing adult. Sports influence girls' physical health, psychological well-being, overall social development and academic achieve-ment.

Girls have a difficult time these days — many have overwhelming concerns about their competence, self-worth and body image. Regular participation in exercise and sport programs provides tangible ex-periences of achievement that teach girls problem solving skills and promote self-confidence. Through the influence of healthy role models and interaction with teammates, young athletes learn how to deal with failure and how to create expectations of success.

Involvement in sports and the development of an identity as an athlete help a young girl to get through the everyday stresses by increasing self-esteem, low-ering tension, and teaching her how to better handle challenges. Being physically active helps to create a healthy body image. Being an athlete also encourages girls to avoid risky actions and learn responsible social behaviors. It can also be an antidote to such social problems as teen pregnancy, substance abuse and violent behaviors.

Sports are an educational asset in girls' lives. Research findings show that high school female athletes report higher grades and lower drop-out rates and are more likely to go on to college than their non-athlete counterparts. Team sports and the competitive arena are a natural place to learn the lessons of positive conflict resolution. The universal character of sport helps to break down barriers, challenge stereotypes and act as a tool for tolerance.

General Discussion Questions:

What do you think makes playing sports fun?

Who are your heroes in sports?

What makes her/him special?

What do you need to be good at sports?

How do you get ready to play your sport?

What do you worry about when you play sports?

What is the most important part of playing your sport?

How important is winning?

Would you do anything to win?

Women's Fencing

There are more opportunities for women fencers than ever before. Fencing for girls and women can range from local clubs for instruction and competition to world championships and the Olympics at the elite level. Sometimes, fencers will compete in all of the events — foil, épée and sabre. But most fencers choose to improve their skills in only one weapon.

Fencers come in all shapes and sizes. Sharon Monplaisir states, "The qualities that make someone a great fencer are patience, balance, timing and strength." And it can be a lifetime sport, with age group tournaments at all levels.

FENCING PROGRAMS

Junior Olympics: Every year the Junior Olympic Fencing Championships (JOs) are held. These popular events are spread over five categories: under-20, under-17, under-15, under-13, and under-11.

National level: The National Championships are held each year. The USFA selects a National Team each year based on national point standings, or rankings. Fencers can earn points at national and international competitions. The training center for National Women's Foil is The Rochester Fencing Centre in Rochester, NY.

Veterans: Events for Veterans (fencers 40 and over) are held at both the national and international levels.

Wheelchair Fencing: there has been a national wheelchair fencing program since 1994. The very best of these athletes are selected to compete in the Paralympic Games. The first USA wheelchair fencing team competed in 1996 at the Paralympics in Atlanta.

RESOURCES:

Resources for girls and women's sports and fitness information:

The Women's Sports Foundation:
www.womensportsfoundation.org

Just Sports for Women website:
www.SportsforWomen.com

The Melponeme Institute website:
www.melponeme.org

GirlPower!Sports & Fitness:
www.health.org/gpower/girlarea/sports

Resources for fencing information:

United States Olympic Committee:
www.usoc.org/sports

The USOC now has a link on their website called, "Where Do I Play?" which will list clubs in your area.

United States Fencing Association:
www.usfa.org

If you are interested in finding a local program, this is another resource

Black Women in Sport Foundation:
www.mcsgnet.com/bwsf

This organization offers fencing programs to inner-city girls in eight states

A Brief History
of Women's Fencing

1888: Women began fencing at private clubs
1896: Fencing is included in the first Olympic Games in Athens — men only
1912: Adelaide Baylis wins the first women's foil National Championships
1924: Women's foil becomes an Olympic event
1929: The Intercollegiate Women's Fencing Association (IWFA) is founded
1955: First women's foil event at the World Under-20 Championships
1957: Electric foil is used for the first time at the National Championships
1968: The first woman to carry the U.S. flag into Opening Ceremonies is six-time Olympic fencer Janice Lee York Romary
1981: Sue Badders wins the first women's épée at National Championships
1989: Women's épée is first held at the World Championships
1996: Women's épée is added to the Olympic Games

Glossary

Allez: (ah-lay) the official word that tells the fencers to begin the bout

Abandoned: left all alone; no body living there

Amateur: a person who does something for enjoyment, not money

Anatomy: the science that studies different parts of the body

Ancient: having to do with times long past

Attack: a movement by which the fencer tries to score a point against his/her opponent

Bout: a timed, scored match in competition

Breeches: short, baggy pants; part of the fencing uniform

Challenge: something that takes a lot of effort

Charred: made black from burning

Counterattack: an attack move made in response to your opponent's attack

Decathlon: a track and field competition in which each athlete takes part in 10 events

Determination: having your mind set on reaching a goal without giving up

Double-cross: to disappoint someone by doing the opposite of what is promised

Dueling: a fight between two people with weapons

En-garde: the position taken before the bout begins; the ready position

Épée: (epp-pay) a fencing weapon with a straight, flexible blade, heavier and stiffer than the foil; it is a thrusting weapon

Fencing: the sport of fighting with swords

Fluorescent: a cool light from a tubular bulb

Foil: a fencing weapon with a straight flexible steel blade, weighing less than a pound; it is a thrusting weapon

Focus: to direct your attention to something

Gauntlet: the padded glove that covers half the forearm

Goddess: a female superhuman being worshipped as having great powers

Grip: the handle of the weapon

Hilt: the handle of the sword where you hold the weapon

Hit: what you score by touching the opponent's target area with the point of the weapon; one hit equals one point; see "touch"

Hitchhike: to travel by asking for a ride from strangers

Inspiration: a positive influence or example

International: between several countries

Instinct: an ability you are born with; something you know without being taught

League: a number of teams joined together in a group

Limber: having a flexible body that moves with quickness and ease

Lunge: the movement where a fencer gets closer to his/her opponent by moving the front leg forward while the back leg stays still; the most common attack

Musty: having a stale smell

Opponent: the person you compete against in a contest

Parry: an action made to protect from attack by blocking the opponent's blade

Piste: the fencing strip, or area, 14-meters long by two-meters wide; the fencer must be on the piste for the hit to count

Podium: a stand on the stage that holds the speaker's microphone and notes

Praying mantis: a large insect that holds its legs as if praying

Pommel horse: a piece of equipment used in gymnastics

Riposte: an offensive action that may be delayed or immediate

Saber: a fencing weapon with a straight flexible steel blade; the touches are made with a cutting edge

Scholarship: a gift of money to a student to help pay for school

Solitary: being alone

Stammer: to speak in an unsure way, often stopping or repeating sounds

Strategy: a plan

Technique: a way of performing or doing something

Tension: nervous feeling, stress

Torso: the human body, not including the head, arms or legs

Touch: what you score by touching the opponent's target area with the point of the weapon; one touch equals one point

Tournament: a series of contests trying to win the championship

Thrust: a lunge to try a touch with the point of your weapon

Trudge: to walk with effort

Warrior: a person who fights in wars

About the Authors

Dr. Doreen Greenberg is a certified consultant in sport psychology and has worked with school, college, professional and Olympic athletes from a variety of sports. These experiences have ranged from consulting with national and world champions to helping young children with their initial fears about training and competition. Dr. Greenberg was a primary author of *Physical Activity and Sport in the Lives of Girls* (1997), a report for the President's Council on Physical Fitness and Sports; an Associate Editor of *The Encyclopedia of Women and Sport in America* (Oryx Press, 1998); and Editor of *Sport in the Lives of Urban Girls* (Women's Sports Foundation, 1998).

Michael A. Greenberg is a former English teacher and retired business executive. While going to college in the Boston area in the late 1960's, he attended every Sixers-Celtics game at the old Boston Garden. Unfortunately, he was supposed to be attending classes at the time.

Michael and Doreen have two grown daughters and live at the New Jersey shore with their three dogs.

Did You Enjoy This Book?

Be sure to look for other titles in the *Anything You Can Do ...* series:

A Drive to Win: The Story of Nancy Lieberman-Cline
(isbn: 1-930546-40-8)

Sword of a Champion: The Story of Sharon Monplaisir
(isbn: 1-930546-39-4)

And coming in 2001:

Fast Lane to Victory: The Story of Jenny Thompson
(isbn: 1-930546-38-6)

Gold in Her Glove: The Story of Julie Smith
(isbn: 1-930546-37-8)

For information about these and other quality Wish Publishing titles, check out our website:
www.wishpublishing.com